Christian Clip Art Volume I

Finally! An easy way to show all kinds of people you care! Instructional Fair's **Christian Clip Art Volume I** contains 48 pages packed with beautiful Christian art that is perfect for so many activities and occasions.

You can use the many pictures of angels, crosses, the Bible, praying hands, Jesus, Mother and child, flowers, children, parents, butterflies and much, much more in a variety of ways. Use them on your newsletters, monthly notes, reminders, invitations or as rewards for children.

Also included in this book are borders, writing paper and awards—all of which enable you to easily show others your appreciation of their hard work and will help you communicate the joy of teaching in a Christian environment.

All the art contained in this book is printed on one side only so clipping directly from the book does not interfere with something on the back of the page. You may wish, however, to photocopy what you need so you will have a complete page to use again.

So, now you can relax when it comes time to be creative, because with our fantastic clip art book, all the hard work is done. Just clip or copy and enjoy!

1

MCMXCIV Instructional Fair, Inc.

3

6

7

8 MCMXCIV Instructional Fair, Inc.

12

MCMXCIV Instructional Fair, Inc.

Vacation
Bible
School

Smile
God Loves
You!

13

Welcome to Sunday School!

HAND IN HAND

A wall display!

1. Attach letters:
   REACH OUT AND TOUCH
   SOMEBODY'S HAND,
   MAKE THIS A BETTER WORLD
   IF YOU CAN!
   to hall or classroom wall.
2. Have each student trace one hand on construction paper and cut out.
3. Attach hands in rows — touching.

REACH OUT AND TOUCH SOMEBODY'S HAND

MAKE THIS A BETTER WORLD IF YOU CAN!

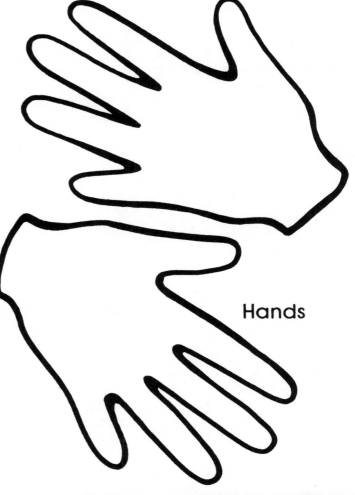

Hands

I've been a little angel today

I've Been a Little Angel Today

18

God Made Me Special!

God Made Me Special!

"I am the good shepherd." John 10:14

head

To Make:
Use an opaque projector to enlarge patterns on white posterboard. Outline features with black marker. Attach patterns to a piece of posterboard. (See illustration.) Use as a door or hall decoration, or in the classroom.

hoof (Make 4.)

tail

LOVE ONE ANOTHER

God Made Me Special!

Jesus Loves

PRAYER IS LOVE

GOD MADE Me SPECIAL!

God Made Me Special!

God Made Me Special!

Jesus LOVES me!

LOVE

MCMXCIV Instructional Fair, Inc.

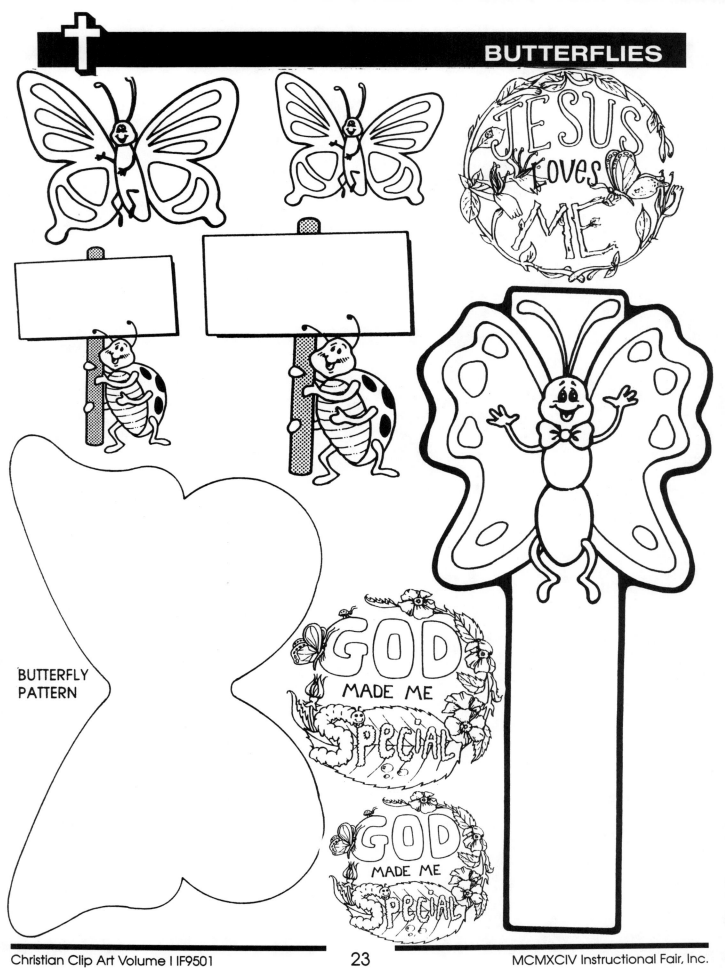

BUTTERFLY
PATTERN

MCMXCIV Instructional Fair, Inc.

"*Love one another.*" John 15:12

PROMISE

REJOICE

REJOICE

JESUS loves ME

Jesus loves Me

PRAISE!

JOY

Jesus loves Me

FLOWER PATTERN

paper
flowers

Love
is
patient.

Love
your
neighbor.

Love
is
kind.

Love
one
another.

Popsicle
sticks

God
is
Love.

clay
flower
pot

"Be glad
in the Lord."

Psalms 104:34

FLOWER

"To everything there is a season,
and a time to every purpose
under heaven."

Ecclesiastes 3:1

"May the Lord bless you and keep you."

Numbers 6:24

SUN

SMILE, GOD LOVES YOU!

30

31

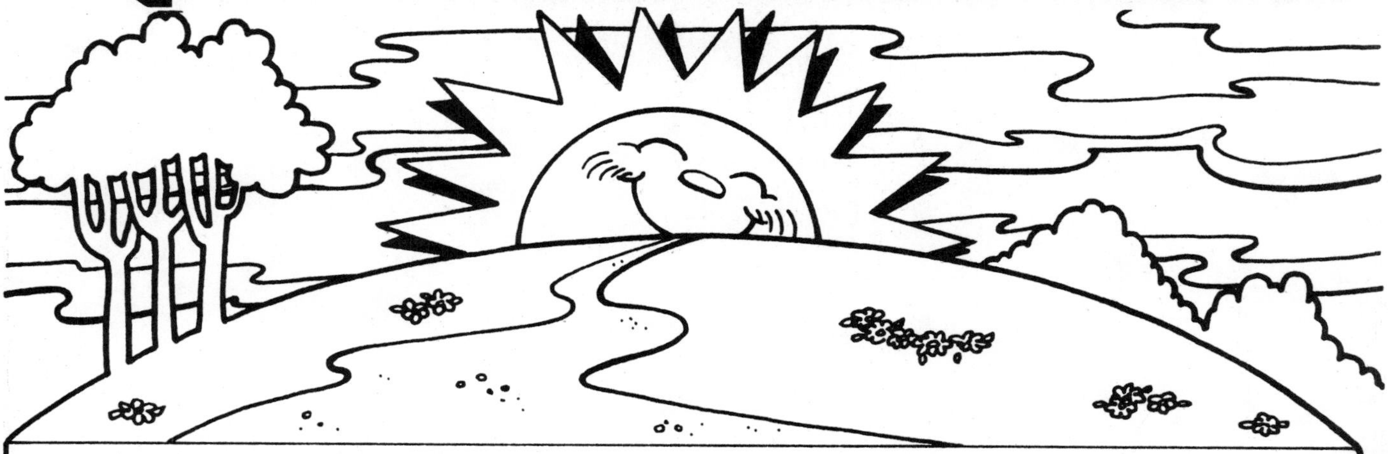

36

MCMXCIV Instructional Fair, Inc.

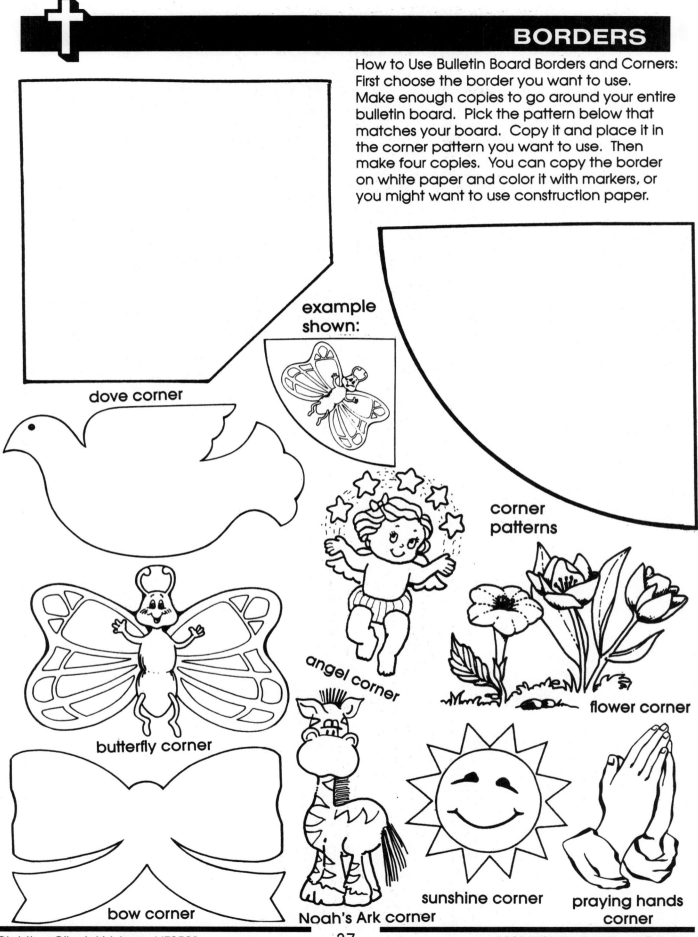

BORDERS

How to Use Bulletin Board Borders and Corners:
First choose the border you want to use.
Make enough copies to go around your entire
bulletin board. Pick the pattern below that
matches your board. Copy it and place it in
the corner pattern you want to use. Then
make four copies. You can copy the border
on white paper and color it with markers, or
you might want to use construction paper.

dove corner

example shown:

corner patterns

angel corner

flower corner

butterfly corner

bow corner

Noah's Ark corner

sunshine corner

praying hands corner

38

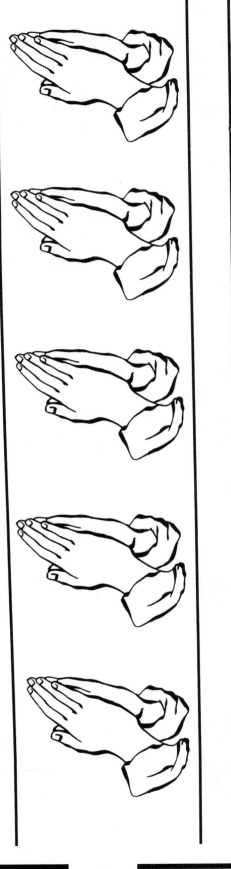
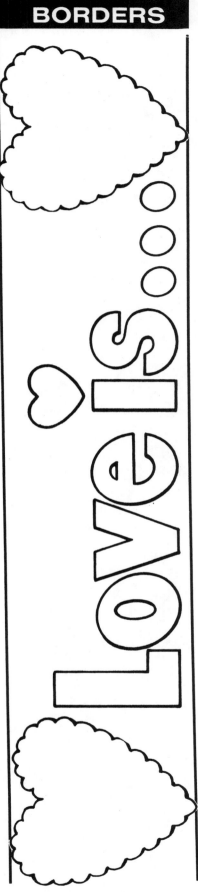

39

MCMXCIV Instructional Fair, Inc.

PARENT APPRECIATION

Certificate

signed

date

SHINING STAR AWARD

name

for shining in

signed   date

Good Faith Award

name

signed   date

"Have faith in the Lord our God . . ." 2 Chronicles 20:20

name   date

Happy Birthday

signed

"Sing to the Lord . . ." **Psalm 98:1**

Bible Memory Award

Holy Bible

name

has memorized the bible verse

signed   date

"I will praise the Lord with all of my heart . . ." **Psalm 138:1**

Lamb of God

Given to _____

For _____

Date _____

Signed _____

"I am the good shepherd; I know my sheep . . ." John 10:14

Kindness Award

_____
name

for showing kindness
to others

_____   _____
signed   date

"Be kind to one another . . ." Ephesians 4:32

Good Citizenship
Certificate

Given to _____

For _____

Date _____

Signed _____

"Love one another . . ."
John 15:12

PEACE

_____
name

for
working well with
others

_____   _____
signed   date

"My peace I give you . . ."

John 14:27

GRADUATION

Given to _____

For _____

Date _____ Signed _____

"Teach me thy way, O Lord . . ." **Psalms 86:11**

PROMOTION CERTIFICATE

_____
name

congratulations for successfully completing

_____

_____   _____
signed   date

"Follow what is good . . ." **1 Thessalonians 5:15**

Perfect Attendance

In Celebration

Given to _____

For _____

_____   _____
signed   date

"Be glad in the Lord . . ." Psalms 104:34

48